The Safety Salesman – Shoot From The Lip

Simon Neil JONES

Foreword

Jimmy Quinn

The Safety Salesman – Shoot From The Lip

Contents

Foreword

Here goes.

I have known Simon since the start of lockdown and noted that he is very similar to me, or me to him, in the way that we both think. He has created a funny, articulate book that looks inside what he is all about. It will make you think and smile.

Health and Safety isn't a calling. It is a job. A role and appointment where people speak sense and create workable solutions that involve other people.

It involves looking at the "grey" areas, moving forwards and developing, mentoring and supporting the lessons learnt. In this book questions are asked and sometimes no answers given, but that's your job.

To read.

To think.

To agree.

Or to disagree.

Although thinking is the thought behind it all.

This pocketbook of puns, honesty, quotes and questions is a gold mine of transparency and learning from someone who looks at Health and Safety through the same lens as me. It is funny, tongue in cheek but with a balanced and respectful narrative. Like Simon, and me it's "formally informal and informally formal". Work that one out.

A book of how life and growing up has given Simon the knowledge, personality and resilience to do what he has done, with some sadness, a smile on his face, a thirst for knowledge and above all a dedication to support people and see them succeed.

Read it.

Enjoy it.

SEE what Simon is saying.

Health and safety are words that we have grown up with as people.

Maybe it's time to associate these words more with respect, honesty, loyalty and understanding.

Jimmy Quinn Immediate Past President IOSH, Veteran Ambassador and Multiplex Plc Senior Health and Safety Manager

Introduction

OK.

So, before we start, this is my first ever go at this book-writing thing so go easy on me. We're in bucket list territory here. I've hit the 4th decade of my life and just getting around to this now. And let me say this to you from the outset. If you're thinking of having a go yourself then do it. Don't overthink it. Don't over analyse it. Don't put if off until next year. Just do it.

This is a bit of theme of the book. I know I know. Just Do It - The "Nike" phrase. But just do it sort of just does it doesn't it? Repeat that back to me.

Tie up your tongue with a twister of a tale...

But enough of that. What I'm trying to say, as I actually do say later on is, don't wait for your ship to come in. Not going to spoil that chapter and tell you anymore because it's a good one and a personal favourite. So you'll just have to read on, or skip straight to it. But then you'd be missing out. So don't.

You get the gist.

A bit about me then before we get into it.

The backstory if you like.

I had no real idea what I wanted to do when it came to thinking about proper jobs, so I went to university back when there were no fees. If it was like it is now, there's probably no way I'd have gone. I spent 3 years in Leeds learning some life lessons, a bit about history and politics and a lot about going out and then it was time to think about proper jobs again. I knew what I didn't want to do and basically wanted a job with loads of action and excitement.

Some of my university pals went onto careers in the military and I had a look at that, but I really, really don't like being told what to do (typical Aries), so found the Army officer selection process not for me.

And also I hate running.

My eyesight isn't great, and I couldn't afford to pay to become a private pilot, so that was out too. A few of my mates went on to study law, but at the time, that just didn't really speak to me either. Policing looked quite good though and didn't involve as much running...

Fast-forward a year and that's where I ended up. And that was me for 13 years. I spent time in uniform, plain clothes, the CID and in some specialist units. My police career ended early though, and I was left with PTSD and retired on medical grounds at the grand old age of 35. And that was tough. Proper tough. And I'll be honest it took its toll on me and those closest to me. But, as the time goes by, we're getting there again and healing. I had about a year and a half off after policing to start to piece myself back together and plenty of time to think about what I did and didn't want to do next.

And I still hated running.

A friend put me in touch with a couple of great guys who owned and ran a small safety training company, and they were on the lookout for instructors. They took me on and looked after me for a while. If they are reading this then they know who they are, and I am forever grateful to them for giving me a chance. Re-invention and rehabilitation is hard and it really helps to have people around you to support with this.

So, if you've been through it or are going through it, you know you need good people around you. I was lucky. I had them at home and at work. Not saying I didn't put in the hours to make it happen, but the support was always there. Important point.

So having "fallen" into safety, like a lot of people I guess, I got another break at a local College who took me on as their H&S Manager. Again, a guy there took a chance on me, and I told him I wouldn't let him down. I didn't. I worked with a lot of good people there and it was a really rewarding experience. The Facilities Team in particular were top people and I learnt loads. It was a great time to be there because they were just building a new campus, so I spent my time teaching myself construction safety and asking loads and loads of questions.

I had a couple of moves after that to keep stretching myself, made one bad move but still used it to learn stuff and another that showed and proved to myself that I had loads of transferrable skills and what 5-star safety looked like. I wanted a head of department role, and an opportunity came up in a small family-run business that was growing fast so I took it. Fast forward another 4 years and here we are. Multi-award winning, funny letters after my name, an amazing team built from scratch and some of the most rewarding professional work I've ever done.

And I still hate running...

Joking aside though, I guess as much as I always knew what I didn't want to do and the need for action did eventually pass, I always found looking out for people rewarding. Working shifts is OK when you're single or even when you're young and married and can sleep in the day. Not so much when there are babies around. And Mrs. J and I (as she says I am partly responsible) decided to have three. And at one stage, had three under three years old. Yes, it was like living in a zoo. So not doing that anymore and sleeping at night and not working at weekends is actually quite nice.

The idea to start writing all came about from an interview I was doing to support a great guy who was doing a research paper and a question I was asked about effective ways to improve standards. So, after a bit of waffle from me about getting buy in and people on board, I started talking about not being the "boring safety person no-one wants to talk to" and instead start thinking about ways in which you can add value.

To do this you have to be able to understand a bit about what it is that people do, how the company or organisation you work for makes money or what the really important things are that you can influence and add value to. That way and then by having little conversations about safety, quality or whatever else the other support functions outside of the main operation do, you can start to try and change things and then "sell" some of these ideas. Being effective in this safety business is essentially like being in a sales job. But you're selling something that nobody wants to buy or thinks they don't want to buy.

Pause on that a moment and see if it makes sense.

If it does then, great. This IS the book for you.

Safety has such a bad rep. And a lot of it is due to what as an industry or "profession" it has done it to itself. So many people I think are turned off by it because it's presented as boring, long winded, bureaucratic and often extremely complex. But it doesn't have to be like that. I really don't think of myself as a traditional "safety person" and I find safety actually pretty interesting. Yes, said that too. Safety is actually pretty interesting. Quote me.

I've worked with some great people, in some brilliant organisations and done some work that I'm really proud of in the safety field, so it doesn't have to be and shouldn't be a turn off for people. And whilst I'm at it, we've got to start to get young people into this game as well, but we'll talk about that a bit later too.

So, I'm saying to you add value and sell safety by helping people solve problems.

Examples?

Do simple things like rather than confuse people with how much legislation you know, instead interpret it and help people out.

Show and present easy to understand things like templates they can follow and standardise stuff, so everyone is doing the same thing.

Get risk assessments in a format that people can actually understand and have at least a fighting chance of someone actually reading.

Less is more.

Seriously, I've investigated some heavy crimes with less paperwork than some basic safety stuff I've seen.

Look into how technology and IT systems can help out and make some of this really easy. There are some great applications and software out there now (no plugs) but go and check them out.

Look and show the value behind proactive work like site audits, not just in terms of accident reduction or prevention, but also really sell the idea of how they can add value to a business and what good safety does for the bottom line, reputation and client feedback. You know, all the good stuff that the commercial types talk about.

Why?

Because this can open the doors to future work and business. Yes, I said it. Safety is a HUGE commercial issue. If it wasn't then it wouldn't be pretty much the first thing any new potential clients ask for on any tender applications or qualifying questionnaires now, would it?

Perhaps, because this safety thing for me is a second career, far removed (at least I used to think) from my previous one, that this is the reason why I don't see myself as a typical safety person. Perhaps not. I don't know. But I will be frank with you. If you do seriously want to actually get anything done and make a REAL difference, then you can't be the clipboard toting, high-viz jacket wearing person, who can quote legislation or regulations and just tell people they are doing stuff wrong.

Don't be that person.

Instead, be somebody who adds value. Be the go-to person for that instead. And to do this it's about selling and not telling.

This is what I've always looked to do. And I hope some of what I go on about in this book helps you to do the same.

Safety is really important, so you have to get it right. But you don't get taught how to be effective at it in any qualification. And for me this is a mistake. To be effective, learning how to talk and speak to people at all levels should be high on the agenda for future skills development and learning. Management skills and call it "operational or commercial understanding" also has to be included if you are going to have the biggest impact.

I played around with a few titles for this book and had always been leaning towards something about selling rather than telling safety, as this was, after all a key theme and I had the whole "Safety Salesman" idea going on from a few blogs I'd done previously anyway.

However, Mrs. J, who always likes to wade in at the last minute and make sweeping changes to our life decisions (examples - paint colour for walls, position of the windows in the extension, how many dogs and/or children we'd agreed to have), "suggested" that this didn't really sound that interesting (straight to the point) and I needed to develop it a bit.

My dear friend KC also bluntly said that my alternative title was "rubbish" (even straighter to the point), so "we" collectively went with what we've got here in the full title.

I guess what I'm trying to say with it is that I'm going at this from the straight to the point angle, telling it like it is (to me anyway) and using the ideas more associated with sales than safety so, "Shoot From The Lip" seemed like a good idea (again to me anyway).

I hope by the end of it you get an understanding of where I'm coming from and if you feel the same way, you can take something away and do something of your own with it.

Before we get started properly then, it's a massive thanks to some people that have already had a little mention and some others that really influenced and guided me. So let's name some names.

Alan for getting me the first break when things were looking dark. Top fella.

Gordon and Brian for taking me on, and let's face it, based on Alan's recommendation and then looking after me when I was fragile. Stevie H also in here because he is a genuine bloke. He knows the score and enjoys a dirty burger. He gets it. If you've had one. You will too.

Robin, Rob and Alan (same name, different person) from Wirral Met for again taking a chance on me and letting me be me.

KC for enduring me and being an all-round good egg. Very proud of you. Keep going.

Ross from Glasgow Caledonian University for inspiring me to have a go at this. He'll play it down of course, but it was after speaking to him that the old light bulb moment went off (or is it on?) for me and I finally plucked up the courage to write a bit and then a bit more on some of my thoughts, rather than just talk to myself on the way home from work about this stuff (in between calls to Mrs. J of course, about what we're having for tea, how her day has been, the kids, the dogs, but mainly about what we're having for tea). Thanks man.

My pal Rich for being there for me because it's not all about work. Relentless...

Karen, who is a proper author and someone you should go and check out. A genuine and kind guiding light, that helped me pull all this together at a vital point and get it over the line and in front of you.

Jim, for lending his (very) good name to all this. Also, his time and effort to write a foreword that is amazing. I couldn't have asked for anything or anyone better.

And of course, Mrs. J and the three bin lids - HBK. They will feature throughout. This is for them after all.

And to all the others that have inspired, conspired and retired along the way... I raise a glass, tip my hat, wink and salute you.

The Safety Salesman.

Chapter 1 - Be Legit

So, we're kicking this off then with a bit about being real. True to yourself. You know, legit. You could say authentic if you want. You've got to be yourself and have your own style. And this will develop and change a bit over time, as you grow older.

Getting older is OK. I had a bit of a wobble with it a few years ago, but we're good now. The hair gets thinner, and the body gets thicker. That's it. No big deal. The journey is what it's all about.

Who you are though, what it is that makes you, you, is really important to try and understand. Some people get it straight away. Others take a bit longer. I like to think of myself as a work in progress. Some bits I've got down cold. Some bits need a tinkering with. A little bit here and there needs an overhaul...

And I will probably never be the "finished" article.

I reckon Michael Angelo (the guy that painted that big ceiling, not the ninja turtle) was thinking something like that when he looked up at his work.

(Thinking in Italian)

"It's good. Like really good. OK it's a masterpiece but if I just put another dab of paint here or a little angel over there it might be even better..."

I could be wrong of course and he may have thought it was boss from the start. End of.

What do I know about painting?

I know that painting the hall, stairs and landing is quite enough for me thank you.

Who was your favourite ninja turtle by the way?

I'm saying in the cartoon it's going to be "Michael Angelo". In the movies it's "Raphael". (The original movie from the 90's of course).

There is a point to all this, I promise.

You'll get used to all the pop culture, movie and film references.

What can I say? MTV generation.

Anyway.

Ask any sales types what it takes to be really good at selling and most will tell you that it's about believing in what you're selling. It could be a car, a service, whatever. Simon SINEK (the guy from the TED talks) reckons if you really believe in what you are selling then the words that you use will sound more authentic.

Not heard of Simon SINEK?

Then you should read more.

Anthony WILSON said that once you know. He was making some speech about Zeus flying too close to the sun or something. I sort of like it and made it fit here.

Total legend by the way.

No, not Zeus. Although he was technically was a legend.

Anthony H WILSON.

"The Hacienda", "Joy Division" and "New Order". "Factory Records" and "The Wheel of Fortune". All in one lifetime too. Should have signed "The Smiths".

Amazing.

Steve COOGAN plays him in the movie "24 Hour Party People".

Not heard of Anthony WILSON, Steve COOGAN or "24 Hour Party People"?

Then I just can't help you. And you've wasted your life.

You really should get out more...

I'm messing with you.

Seriously though.

It's all about building relationships and trust.

People buying into what you're saying or trying to do and therefore buying into YOU.

And you get this by being legit.

Yes, get the knowledge, the technical bits and the experience as you go.

Do the courses and the qualifications. Learn on the job. But, as you're doing this always be legit and look to do the right thing by people.

This takes a bit of work. Doing the right thing isn't always easy. There will be times when you may get really tested with this.

Let's look at a couple of scenarios.

Bending the rules or standards because of commercial pressure.

Certified as certain to happen or be said to you at some point during any safety career is something like this,

"Can we let this subby on just this once as it's only a quick job?"

 Or

 "They haven't got the certificates we need but they promised that they'll get them".

Or even a personal favourite of mine,

"They'll do this job for us and then if it goes well, they've said they'll get what we want for next time".

Essentially being held to ransom by your supply chain. Awesome.

So, what are you going to do with these?

Bend the rules?

Break the rules?

Let it happen once and hope this never comes up again?

Good luck.

This is test of being legit and believing in what you're doing and that it is the right thing to do. People will always look for a weak point in the armour and if they find it, they will go for it time after time.

Don't let that happen.

Be resolute and maintain standards.

Now perhaps from what you've read so far, you were not expecting the hard stance here, but this is all part of the selling safety approach. Set the stall out early and get selling. It's a quality product people. Nothing cheap and nasty here. You've worked too hard and got too many of those funny letters after your name to let that be undone by taking decisions that will ultimately and in the end, undermine you or any system or process you are trying to build, maintain or introduce.

So don't do it.

You have been told.

Here's another scenario.

Looking ace on paper but what you really know, is that what goes on at site level is nowhere near it.

A common issue.

There are many classic works of fiction out there in the tender/bid writing world. We really don't need any more, so don't become part of it.

There is nothing wrong at all with showcasing, if what you do is good and then leveraging it for commercial gain (more on this a bit later because it is a key skill to master if you want to add value), but don't say you're doing stuff you're not. At some point you will get found out.

I've written loads of tenders, bids, reports and award submissions that really sell the idea of good safety. This is always backed up though with the one thing that makes it legit.

Evidence.

Go and make sure you are doing what you say you doing by checking and recording it.

We'll talk some more on this as well, as for me it is the most important bit in the old plan do check act model thing.

Check.

Check.

And keep checking.

And if you can do the checks and use some of the latest tools out there (no name dropping/branding support going on here, but there are some great products out there), then take pictures to support your check or your audit/inspection as well. This is really good evidence.

A picture paints a thousand words, yes?

"Michael Angelo".

See?

There is a link to it after all.

What better way to show what you say you are doing than with a consistent, auditable, transparent system of inspections that show the standards week in week out?

Share them with clients, your supply chain or even your insurer.

They will love it.

Sell it.

I have to tell you this.

There is a great line in the movie, "Heat".

The one with Robert De NIRO and Al PACINO in it. And Val KILMER, who is also ace and is the "Ice Man".

We'll have a "Top Gun" reference later.

The guy that plays "Bubba" in "Forrest Gump" (yes, it is him, he's just got some funny fake teeth or gums in) is in this scene where they are chasing down De NIRO'S crew of baddies. They have Val KILMER'S wife in sort of a bit of a bind, as she's got to give him up or go to the slammer herself for assisting him.

Anyway, he's giving her the options, which aren't really much at all, and she asks him,

"What else are you selling?"

And he replies proper deadpan,

 "All kinds of shit. But this shit sells itself".

Killer line that, in a killer movie.

And it does by the way.

Get (sh)it right and it does sell itself. So be legit.

Being legit isn't always about being staunch though. You have to want to make this work.

We're talking selling safety here after all.

It is so easy in the safety game to say no to things. It's a big reason why there is so much bad press about the job (and a lot of it deserved).

Fun Police.

Listen.

You have to start to try and get people to buy into you. So, start to try and look to make decisions, based on good sound advice that supports and facilitates the areas or sectors that you work in and take a risk-based approach.

Sell don't tell.

You have to think a bit like all of the other people, in all the other departments and start to understand them and then look to become effective at selling your message if this is going to work.

Finance, Operations or even our friends in HR.

Hey!

I can say that because I've got the people badge as well you know and they really aren't that bad when you get to know them.

Who would win in the most hated department at work contest?

H&S or HR?

I'm joking.

We all know its HR.

Remember.

Good sales is all about knowing a product inside and out and believing in it. That way people buy into it and you. So, get to know the business, the other people in it, what they do and how they do it.

Lots of open questions there.

Remember what an open question is?

The big ones that achieve a wider answer than a simple yes or no.

So, if I asked you,

"Is it raining outside?"

You could tell me either yes or no. I wouldn't really learn much and the conversation could be over.

But if I asked you something like,

"What's the weather like outside?"

Or even better,

"Tell me what the weather is like outside".

Then I'm more likely to get a broader, more expansive answer from you that helps me learn more.

These are your what, why, where, who, when and how questions.

Really, really, good skills to learn when you come to talk people.

And taking this approach then means getting out and learning what goes on and how things work.

You have to be willing to learn in this game if you want to get on. It will help you.

So, you'll end up knowing a bit or maybe quite a bit about every aspect of a business or organisation. You'll pretty much meet everyone and get to know them, or at least know of them.

No silo working here.

If you are, or feel like that, then something is wrong.

Change that.

It also means pretty much everyone knows you too, or of you at least, so you have to be comfortable with that. This is, and should be a high-profile role, so getting your pitch right is really important.

Let's talk about credibility while we're here then too.

So, you're working on keeping the standards and quality up?

Good work.

You're starting to think about getting out and checking what is going on?

Ditto.

And you reckon that you know at least a little bit about what that guy in the far office does over the other side of the site?

Excellent.

So, let's look at credibility then and how to develop it.

OK, this is a tough one as you only really get one go at this, so if you get this wrong or make a wrong call your credibility can walk.

Difficult.

However, we eat difficult for breakfast, don't we?

We don't really though.

I like. No, I love, by the way. A full English breakfast.

And I reckon I could eat a full English every day. No sweat.

And I probably would if:

      a)   I had the time

      b)   Mrs. J wasn't on my case.

Credibility though.

We have to be careful. It's on the line from day one, especially if you're new in a role. All the eyes are on you. Some of those eyes are looking to see where the gaps in the armour are and to test you.

We can see them coming.

Some are looking to see if you're a pain and as bad as that lot in HR.

Again, we can deal with them. Worst-case scenario with this one.

Team up with HR and beat them all.

Joking.

Never team up with HR.

Really though.

There will come a time, probably early on too if you're new in a role especially, that a credibility issue will come up. Do not be afraid of this but do be prepared for it.

I say this when it comes to gaining credibility with others.

Be right and be consistent.

This is something I tell every one in my team in the first instance.

And when I say be right, I'm talking about those funny letters and stuff after your name and the work you've put in to get there.

The Knowledge.

Not easy this game and there is LOADS to learn. No way that you'll ever know it all either. This is also what it makes it good, as there is always something to be learning.

You've done some learning, so don't be afraid to use it and add value.

Important bit though.

If you don't know. Say you don't.

Never give some half-baked answer or make up some imaginary law or something like the, "As and When Act". Someone will find out and you will be done. Trust gone.

Say instead, that you'll go and find out the answer and come back to them. And then do it. This is not a weakness. This is being legit.

Be consistent too with any advice.

This goes back to the bit on having standards and quality.

 Don't tell one person one thing and one person another, because guess what?

People talk.

And they will.

And if the messages are different, then you will become undermined and this is no good.

One consistent message is the way forward.

And that's it. Chapter 1 done and dusted.

Be legit.

To get this safety thing right, it's as much about selling (something that people don't want or think they don't want, remember), as it is about anything else.

Plenty of time and room for a chat about the Heinrich triangle or the Swiss Cheese model if you want but not right here. We're all about selling safety so let's get on with it.

Chapter 2 - Invest In People

So, you're here then?

Chapter 2.

Well done.

So, you're a seller and not a teller then eh?

Excellent.

When I wrote this bit I was reflecting on a member of my team and friend of mine, being in the final of a big safety awards thing. It was a pretty big deal with a virtual glamourous host and all that, and I really wanted her to win because:

   a) She deserved it

   b) She's earnt it and

c) I wrote the submission and was on a 10% kick back.

Two out of those three are true. You choose...

Seriously though, it was and is a brilliant thing to see other people doing well and really rewarding to have had a small hand in helping them to get to where they want to be.

I've met a lot of people along the way who just want to hold on to all the knowledge and learning they've picked up and not pass anything on. Or help anyone else get to where they want to be or be the best that they can be.

Don't be that person.

Other people knowing what you know isn't a bad thing or a sign that they are going to take your job or something.

It's a pretty well trodden path and idea that the aim when you move on from a job or an organisation, is to leave it in a better place than when you started with it.

This should be the same too for the people that you work with, that work for you and even that you work for.

Make a difference with people.

It feels good and is the right thing to do.

Investing in people doesn't always mean spending loads of money on them either.

But it does mean spending time (and proper time when you are present and not going through the motions) with them.

Get to know a bit about them and give them a bit about you too.

Here's something I picked up when I doing a bit of volunteer broadcasting on our local community radio station a few years ago now.

That's right. On the radio.

Get me.

It was ace and I loved it. I was gutted when I had to finish due to other commitments. If you get the chance or want to do it, then have a go because you'll love it too. I'll be doing it again at some point.

A great memory to share here.

I did this outside broadcast from an estate agents in our local town.

I know.

Estate agents. Rock and roll.

It was during the summer and the tennis was on. Cue Wimbledon theme tune here.

I was a massive 3 weeks into my amateur broadcasting career and had no real idea what I was doing, but it sounded exciting, so I said I'd have a go. You have this little desk with you. See? I don't even know what all the gear is properly called.

You do the talking bit and there is someone else back at the station working the proper desk and playing the tunes. They talk to you and then tell you when the music is coming up and how long you've got left before the music or adverts start. You have to trust them because you can't see the timer thing that counts down when the tunes are starting or how long you've got.

Bottle testing.

Good though.

Anyway, I was doing my stuff and interviewing a couple of the staff and some of the locals from our town, and it was just a great afternoon. I'd retired from the cops at this point and was on the road to recovery, so getting out and about a bit and trying things that pushed me out of my usual comfort zone, was actually really beneficial.

Mrs J popped in with the bin lids (rhyming slang, if you don't get it, you'll work it out), who were really young then and don't remember this at all. And it was just a glorious, surreal thing to be doing at that time in my life. The best compliment was from one of the estate agents' staff who asked me how long I'd been doing it for, and she was properly taken aback when I said 3 weeks!

Literally making it up as I went along.

Don't be afraid of trying something you might not have any real idea about people.

Just have a go. If it goes wrong or isn't quite right the first time, then don't worry.

As the guy who ran the station said once, "It's only radio. No-one died".

Another quick tale about the radio.

Promise.

We'll get back to investing in people in a minute.

We've got this video of our girls at a garden centre when they are about four and five years old. They're just wandering about and, like you do as parents when they're really young, you record everything.

I'm not there as I'm doing a bit on the radio. It just so happens though that they've got the station on and my show is playing through the speakers. The girls hear my voice. Stop for a bit. Recognise it's me, and as I play a song, they do this amazing dance. Proper amazing dance. Never been repeated but captured forever.

Gold.

This is in the archives and memory banks forever.

And it WILL be getting played back at the wedding(s).

A father's prerogative to embarrass the daughter, no?

Absolute Gold.

Investing in people.

What I'm saying is, that the selling bit and the investment in people comes from you.

See?

There is link here somewhere.

OK, maybe not the garden centre story.

That is just a tale that makes me wish time stood still and our girls were still that young.

I am doing my best here and actually thinking about what I'm trying to say to you and give you some rational thoughts...

So, getting back on track.

It helps to get people on board with you and build a foundation of trust, if you can give, even a little about yourself and build rapport. This will bring greater success over time.

It's crazy this, because at the same time I was writing this, I was studying for a Diploma in HR Management myself.

I know!

HR.

Hey OK then, only join with HR if you can be the boss...

Anyway, within the course was a piece on leadership styles and a very interesting idea that works well with what I'm trying to say.

Transformational leadership.

Not up on this?

It's about being proactive, working to change culture, new ideas, motivating others, promoting creativity and innovation and what is this?

Selling and not telling.

And there you have it. It's an actual REAL idea that people study on training courses.

There's also a bit on this thing called "Contingency Theory" by Fred FIELDER. Must reference and give the kudos. Been told.

Hey, if nothing else you're getting an education here, right?

A good point and something to take away though, is about being a people or a task orientated leader and matching your natural style with the needs of a situation.

Pretty decent ideas. You should check them out.

Being relationship motivated then, is about looking to get on with people and using personality to help achieve goals. Therefore, I repeat:

Give a little about yourself and build rapport.

Some of my stuff is even backed up with proper ideas look.

Research, people. Get on it.

So, let's use a sales type of phrase here then to really drive this home.

"Speculate to accumulate".

We really can't expect people to buy into what you're trying to say if there is no investment in them, can we?

We are selling not telling remember.

You can't do this safety game on your own. Let's go bigger than that.

You can get loads more done with other people around you, so remember that.

You have got to get people involved and engaged. People that are engaged and pulling together can-do great things. End of.

Every organisation, company, team, whatever, always says the most important asset they have is their people. So really think about that, because without them, there is no "culture" or "values".

They are just words on the office wall or in some promotional material or website. There literally is no company or organisation without people. They ARE it.

Now, I am not saying that you're going to win everyone over and sell everyone. And if you do think that then, whilst I applaud your optimism, my experience just tells me that this is not a realistic objective.

So don't try and change the world just yet, but never say never, and don't give up.

It doesn't stop you selling mind you.

Just be prepared for not everyone to get it.

Or want to get it.

Remember too, you are selling something that a lot of people don't want or think they don't want, so you are going to get some knock backs.

Some closed doors.

Some "no thanks".

But be resilient and keep going.

"No-one ever said it was going to be easy"

Good tune that by "The Inspiral Carpets".

They had some good tunes.

I missed them the first time really. Lots of organ playing going on.

"The Charlatans" the same.

Not as good as "The Smiths" like. More on them in the next bit.

Closing remarks then, as you've had enough on this.

Invest in people.

Do it properly and do it genuinely.

From yourself.

I'm sure I said something before about being legit...

Go sell it

Chapter 3 - Muck And Bullets

How's it going so far?

Are you getting any of this?

Am I making ANY sense?

Sort of rhetorical questions those that I'm asking myself as I write this.

Suppose it's about connection in the end?

Trying to reach out and get that thing going where you might get a nod or a feeling of,

"Yeah, I understand that".

Relatable. Know what I mean?

What we must all understand and appreciate first off though, is that I think that "The Smiths" are awesome. And you if you agree, then you therefore my friends, are awesome too.

By proxy, awesome.

Music and films, but music mostly, has defined many aspects of my life. Play a certain song and it can instantly bring back a memory or a time in your life. Well it can for me anyway.

"The Smiths" were, and are still, my all time favourite band. And I never even got to see them live, as I was just that bit too young when they were first around. But I do remember hearing them for the first time at school and they blew my mind. And they have been with me ever since. Mrs. J says they are miserable. I say they are ironic. And she likes "Sonia", so what does she know?

A memory to share with you then.

I took my son (and heir).

Stop right there.

Not a sexist comment on lads and girls as I've got both before you start, but merely a little Smiths related pun.

Is it a pun?

Whatever it is, an in-joke then.

LOL. (This means laugh out loud for anyone over 25)

And if you're a Smiths "head", you will of course get it, and if you're not then, I say again, you've wasted your life...

"Hang the DJ".

Anyway, the son and heir got taken to Salford Lads Club in Manchester a few years ago to soak up the atmosphere (alright I'll explain - Salford Lads Club is a famous location for the band and is now a museum – yes, it is a museum, stop laughing) and hang out with some fellow "heads", as I was trying desperately to educate him to have musical taste as good as mine, and not his mother's...

It was very cool.

When I was ten, I wore a "Super Mario" T-Shirt and some kid from another school on a field trip to France took the piss out of me.

My boy at ten had "The Queen Is Dead" on his T-shirt and was sporting a quality quiff at the time. The "heads" loved him.

There really is a "light that never goes out" (you either get it or you don't).

But enough of this.

You've not come here to read my ramblings about bands and T-Shirts, so we will have to discuss why Anthony WILSON should have signed "The Smiths" to Factory Records another time.

To business then my friends. Let's learn something.

So, I was thinking about this bit again during the awards season in the safety world.

Time for reflection these and good for benchmarking.

I'm really in complete free-thinking consciousness mode here by the way as I write this little bit, and will probably do something on the value of awards later on, as it sounds to my brain right here and now like a decent bit to write about.

Insert disclaimer here.

Just in case there isn't a bit on the value of awards and you're looking for it later in the book, as I've thought in the end it was a rubbish idea or, I can't remember what or how I was going to link adding value to it at all because I got distracted thinking about that clever Smiths joke...

I should probably edit that bit out.

Too late.

It's been published and I've missed it in the proof read.

Glitzy, glamourous affairs some of these award's things you know.

Tuxedos and everything. Great recognition for organisations and the people that work to deliver best in class, the gold standard, whatever you want to call it. And they really can make a difference as well to drive performance, benchmark and reflect on where you are and where you want to be, you know.

And it was this, and a great comment about the shiny veneer of a shop window hiding what really goes on behind the scenes (nod to you sir, you know who you are), that made me think that, whilst of course we all want to show off the best bits, we can only really know what's going on by being out on the ground.

On sites, on the shop floor, wherever what goes on, really goes on.

This is being amongst the "muck and bullets".

Great phrase.

Not mine. Not sure who said it first.

Good title for an album though.

Stop it.

Free thinking about bands again.

Concentrate man. These people have paid for this.

Anyway.

Behind the glitz and the glamour of awards it can be gritty, grimy and at times almost soul-destroying work to try and achieve a constant message. But this is where you need to be, or certainly be looking, the majority of the time.

Behind the line.

Amongst the muck and bullets.

As I've said before, the most important bit of the plan, do, check, act, thing if you go in for that, is the "check" bit.

You can have top of the range policies, procedures and all the paperwork you want. You can say you're doing this and that and everything is great if you want. But if you want to really get it right, then get out there and prove it.

And this is the real "check".

Call it an audit, an inspection, a Gemba walk (if you're in to that whole 5S sort of thing).

But if you say you're doing it, then give some real assurance by evidencing it.

Here's a fact.

Have a look at the majority of major accidents and incidents of recent times.

Big organisations with all the badges and accredited systems there are in this game.

Yet still, with major failings resulting in fatalities or significant damage and costs can be attributed to issues that would, or should, have been spotted by having boots on the ground and eyes on what's really happening.

And that's the other thing.

This has to be consistent.

I'm talking daily/weekly stuff here, not just an occasional fly by.

Continual.

And then record it.

Here's another little phrase told to me twenty years ago now...

"If it isn't written down. It didn't happen".

Records. Records. Records.

There are loads of good digital tools available now that make this simple and provide photographic evidence as well. So, if you're not doing this, then get out there and have a look at what's available.

Evidence makes what you are saying real. Make sure you're capturing it.

Now, I'm not saying that by doing this you're never going to have an incident or an accident, because in all of this there are humans involved and sometimes, they just do crazy shit (management term, again different nod to a different sir, but you know who you are also).

But, if you are wanting to sell the idea of safety, and if you've got this far into the book then I reckon you probably are, then it's easier to do that when you can back up what you're saying.

If it isn't written down. It didn't happen.

Remember that.

This is probably a decent place then to talk to you about how to put some of these records and reports together, so that they make sense to someone else reading them and, more importantly, add value.

This is a MASSIVE thing in this approach.

ADDING VALUE.

You have to come back to that all the time.

Add value with what you do and how you do it.

If the idea of safety is a bolt on to make a tender or application look good or the "management system" gets tucked away in some dusty file no-one uses, then it has zero value.

We are not interested in that.

It is not our thing.

We are looking to add and maximise value across everything we do.

Reports and records then.

We know that they are important, so let's look at some ways of selling them better.

There are loads of really good applications out there that can create very quick and very simple (simple by the way is also a key take away) audit and inspection templates and then convert them into pretty decent reports that can be shared with your team(s) or clients, or anyone else who may be interested. You never know when you might need them...

These kinds of records and reports are a great way to evidence what you're doing. The use of IT has been a very successful strategy for me, and I am no whizz on computers I can tell you, but do embrace IT and technology and then prove you are doing what you say you are doing.

To make these kinds of reports really work though, you need a decent template to work from. Again, there are loads of bespoke ones out there, but ask yourself if they really fit the bill for what you're doing?

Better I think to make your own, with input from those people who actually do the job or work that creates the risk.

Hey!

This sounds a bit familiar to me?

That's because it is.

The people you work with, who do the job, are best placed to manage the risk.

Back to basics right here.

Didn't ROBEN'S say that before the old Health and Safety At Work Act first came into being, you safety law geeks?

Rhetorical question again.

He did say that.

Well-read and well fed me, no doubt.

ROBEN'S actual quote then.

"Those that create risk are best placed to manage it".

I've done some homework people. It's not all about bands, movies and ninja turtles...

So, work with these people (those that create risk, not the bands, turtles etc.) and get to know them and understand what is going on.

Your man ROBENS said it, and he kicked this whole thing off with the right approach way back then, so I'm saying it too.

"Those that create risk are best placed to manage it".

Here's just WHY then, that the whole muck and bullets and being amongst it all thing, is so important.

The actual getting out and seeing and "checking" in the right way, what is really going on.

Now, just before we get into this, there is a potentially controversial bit coming up here that may just upset the natural safety educational order and Establishment.

I'm saying it anyway.

Here goes nothing.

"HEINRICH'S Triangle" model doesn't work anymore.

I'm not getting into explaining what this is if you're reading this and don't get this bit. Use that well-known search engine that rhymes with noodle and find out about it.

And frankly, if you are reading a book about safety and you're not in the safety game, you REALLY, REALLY should get out more...

But, for me anyway, to suggest that modelling from data that indicates if you have so many near misses or minor incidents then this is a precursor for a major incident or even a fatality, just doesn't work.

We perhaps could also think about whether a model designed in the 1930's can really relate to the modern world of work, with the mind-blowing technological advancements and speed of everything, and ask if this is really what we should be teaching?

Just my thoughts.

Models, diagrams and theories have a place.

But nothing beats raw intelligence and information.

Straight from the horse's mouth.

The real deal.

The good stuff.

Get off your arse, get out there and see what is really going on.

Plain enough?

I think that's enough on this.

Keep this stuff simple and keep it consistent is the idea. That's the key. That's the sell

Chapter 4 - 50(ish) Shades Of Grey

So, I've got your attention then from the chapter title?

Devious minds think alike, eh?

Tell the truth now.

Did you skip the first three chapters and go straight to this one you cheeky monkeys?

Yes?

You'll be most disappointed then, when I tell you there is nothing of that sort going on here in that department though.

I know. I know.

What a shame.

But listen, we can't have anything too blue, as my Nan will probably read this. She might be the only one who does. Mrs. J doesn't count. And there are already some naughty words in it that will attract a stern look.

What we do have going on here though my friends, is a little bit more on the dark arts of safety, how to sell it, and an idea about compromising and knowing when to move on issues.

I just thought I would jazz it up with a sexy title to get you to read it and get paid (it's an e-book pricing thing that us author types to worry about you know...)

So...

Seeing that you're already here, we might as well just get on with it then, eh?

Read on.

I'm going to talk to you now about how this safety stuff isn't as black and white as you, or maybe some other people, may think it is, with it being a highly regulated and legislated sector.

Yes, there are (lots) of legal bits and pieces and technical stuff that one must get one's head around (posh grammar, I know). But actually, getting anyone to listen or even pay the slightest amount of attention, especially when there are many other distractions in the workplace going on, isn't quite so straightforward.

So you have to pick your moments.

We are talking here then about the shades of grey. And there are MANY more than 50.

So, what on earth do I mean then?

If you go at this stuff with the mind-set that everything you have read or learnt MUST be done to the letter, then you will get literally nowhere. There are humans involved here, so nothing ever survives "first contact".

Operational planning phrase there from the old days.

It goes back to the people sometimes just do crazy shit thing. Go back and read it again if you've forgotten.

Think having a great (I did originally write "boss" here instead of great but was told this is a Scouse phrase that many others do not and would not ever contemplate using, so we went with great instead), well-thought out, top of the range plan, that goes out the window the moment you deploy (again operational planning phrase – substitute "use it") and come into contact with another human.

The plan just comes undone.

Outcomes are not what was intended or planned for.

Steps in a process go out of sequence or missed altogether.

In other words.

It goes to shit.

Note here please.

I know this is another swear word and whilst my Nan may well read this, she will understand. I WILL get the stern look, but it will all be fine. I'll buy her a nice cake.

We, my friends, will speak plainly to each other. We are grown-ups after all. (Also a great film by the way, "Grown Ups". Favourite of Daughter Number 2)

This is normal. (As in plans going wrong is normal and not my Nan giving me a stern look is normal. I was actually a pretty good boy growing up).

You have to learn to live between the lines and adapt a bit. You must use, but sensibly so, a word beginning with "D".

All together now.

"Discretion".

"All Together Now".

A good song that by the band "The Farm."

Proper Scouse football band.

"Terrace Casuals" and all that.

I am digressing here and thinking about Liverpool FC because the mighty "Reds" are on the telly as I'm trying to write...C'mon Red Men.

"Discretion".

Using a bit of discretion is vital and you'll never get any buy in without it. You'll just end up being the safety plod no one wants to talk to and engage with.

Said it before and saying it now.

Don't be that.

You've got to learn a little bit of the old "give and take".

And this is the REAL trick.

And to do it whilst still maintaining the line that isn't to be crossed.

Standards people.

Getting that right is a big win and a top sell.

Not easy and it comes with time, experience and well, just feeling the moment and knowing when to move and when not to.

To do it right you've got to know your stuff first. So don't think this comes without work and lots of it.

If you think about what I've said before, it's all about selling something remember, that a lot of people don't want to buy. Or think they don't. So, you have to sell it to them. And this means working with them and gaining trust, respect and them seeing the value too.

Rules don't really get people to do stuff. People do. And people aren't straightforward.

There are shades of grey around all the time.

Look for them and use them.

There may be occasions when a little chat or a bit of advice will work much better than making a big deal out of something that is relatively minor and can be resolved there and then.

Think about it.

Real life application time then.

You'll have seen no doubt the abundance to behavioural safety stuff that's out there. And for good reason as it's about getting people to think and behave in a way that reflects the ideas (ideals?) of a management system or a standard. No problem with that.

Remember though, all the badges and certificates in the world won't stop someone taking that shortcut, not wearing their PPE or over-riding a system because it's easier, so you have to be out there checking.

But when you are out there and doing a bit, remember that not everything you see has to be taken as a major issue or a non-conformance, to use the "management system" parlance.

Not everything that may be "not quite right" is crime of century.

This is a skill that will come with time and experience and needs to be carefully developed. It's about knowing when to move and when not to.

Jumping all over a minor issue will alienate you and then you've lost.

Think about instead using some coaching methods and talking to people first.

It isn't against the rules to use some humour as well you know.

In fact, it should probably be a pre-requisite in this game.

I'm not saying don't be afraid of raising a flag and waving it if the issue is serious enough or the real risk is there.

Note here.

It is also it's a really good idea to know what your key and real risks are, as this will help you make decisions.

Standby for some more research-based stuff.

Back to the situational leadership idea.

I know.

Research and everything. Well-read and well fed remember?

Insert an emoji thing here of a winking face here to show I am still hip.

Situational leadership anyway…

This is about adjusting your style to meet the needs of a situation, a problem or a group.

One size does not fit all.

This is a good idea and one we can use to our advantage.

Again, go and look this up some more if you want. I'm not here to give you all the answers, but just to signpost you to some stuff that I thought was pretty good and may help you.

You've got to do your own homework people.

I'll give you this though.

With this situational leadership thing, the idea is about flexing styles so you can move and be effective in a given scenario. It uses words like "telling" and "selling" and "participating", so it is definitely something we can look to use.

See what I mean?

We're not re-inventing the wheel here with any of this.

Clever people with degrees and lots of really long funny letters after their names have thought through this before us and created models and named theories after themselves, so it must be worth considering and thinking about.

For me, it's all about the shades of grey and knowing when to move and when not to move.

Trust me.

Think on it a bit and it'll make sense.

Chapter 5 - Talk To Me Goose

If you get the title reference, then congratulations. Your CRUISE-FU is good.

If not, then what HAVE you been doing?

Get searching on that engine that rhymes with noodle and check out a stone-cold classic in "Top Gun".

I reckon I've seen it about 100 times.

Still good.

There's a new one coming out soon. It won't be the same though. They never are. We'll talk some more about sequels later.

There was a time I wanted to be a pilot, as you know.

This idea was based, in the main, on "Top Gun". And at a time when I thought it was basically just all swanning about with Aviators on, riding motorbikes with no helmet and doing a bit of the flying stuff in-between.

Having "crashed and burned" at the flight assessment centre though, I quickly realised Tom and his pals had fooled me and there was quite a bit more to this pilot business, including a heavy involvement of maths, which as my own kids will attest to when we come to do homework, is not my bag.

Plus, I couldn't ride a motorbike.

The swanning about bit I could do though, and looked OK (I thought anyway) in a pair of Aviators...

The point?

Shattered adolescent dreams aside, what we have on display here in this great line of the film is the importance of communication.

"Talk to me Goose", Maverick says.

And when Maverick talks, you listen people. End of.

"It's good to talk".

That catchphrase was used by BT (as in British Telecom) in their adverts in the 90's with Bob HOSKINS. Showing my age here I know and that I watch too much TV (I am a top student of pop culture and you want me on the pub quiz team, trust me).

Movie trivia time again then while we're here.

"Who Framed Roger Rabbit?" and "The Long Good Friday".

Two great films right there starring BH. See what I did there? BT and BH. (No? I thought it was quite clever).

"Roger Rabbit" was groundbreaking at the time of course with the animation and live action and it had "Doc Brown" from "Back To The Future" in it as the creepy baddy judge.

"The Long Good Friday" had a little cameo from a future "James Bond," Pierce BROSNAN. (Told you that you want me on the pub quiz team).

We're talking about communication though.

We HAVE to talk right?

We have to try and reach out to each other, just that little bit more and look for a connection.

Now, I'm not getting all deep and meaningful here on you, but we've all got try a bit harder with this.

There's this phrase called "silo working".

That's about when you work in a job, a role, or even a team or department, and you are disconnected from other teams, departments, or even people and just sort of end up working on your own.

And let me tell you, I've seen loads of this.

It's really quite common in a lot of workplaces.

Sometimes, it's because of simple things, like a team sitting in a separate office or working on a special project so they don't get to talk and communicate with other people as easily. Or, it could be self-imposed because of an attitude or behaviour of a certain group.

Real life example then.

So, for a large part of my police service, I was fortunate enough to work in specialist departments and units, working with some great people and I got to do some amazing things. However, when I reflect on this time now (in part) I wonder if the often, elitist (and it was) attitude of these departments and units, at times made communication with the wider teams and overall objectives of the organisation, actually a bit more difficult than it needed to be.

Perhaps, if communication had been a bit more open, some things could have been achieved better.

Tricky one. And I don't have the answer.

Silos can develop really quickly. People often want to feel part of something and can get properly attached and even inward facing. I'll say insular here. This is especially true if the group is high performing and even aspirational for others.

But I think perhaps, if at times we could have at least have been a bit more aware of this, we could have achieved even more. Purely academic all of this of course and maybe things have moved on a bit since then and attitudes changed. Not sure.

Breaking off for a moment to think here then, and doing the whole free-wheeling conscious writing thing again, reflecting on the good times, the bad times and all the other times in between that gone before.

Do you reflect?

I do and often, especially now I am a bit older.

I find myself not dwelling on the past, but I do like to reflect and at least try and make myself improve and ask questions of whether I could have done things differently or better. And also try and understand why things have not gone to the intended plan sometimes.

Reflection is a good tool I think also to use when planning and well worth taking the time to do.

I've found as I've gone on and progressed, both professionally and personally, that giving myself some time and space in the day to reflect and think is a really good thing. Soak time for the old grey matter to digest and work things out.

I'm a visual person, so I like to have a board on the wall with the ideas on. Broad headings or things I want to achieve. My strategy I suppose. I feel lost without it.

When I moved into a new office and there wasn't one, I had to have one put up so I could spend some time writing things down and then looking at them. Like a big over-arching "To Do" list if you like. I love lists and use them every day just to get stuff done. It's satisfying ticking them off.

And while we're at it then, get yourself a diary as well or a planner, or use a digital one.

I'm old skool (do not correct spell checker) and like a pen and paper diary, but you use whatever you want, but definitely have a look into getting some structure and framework into things. For me it just makes things like time management and getting the most out of each day work.

Hey, maybe this wasn't as much as break from my original ideas on communication as I thought as it was and could be about communication then with yourself.

Profound…

Your inner voice.

We've all got one.

Just re-read that bit back and I'm quite pleased with the end result there.

It just came to me that all that as I was writing.

It's good this writing and reading thing.

REALLY gets you thinking.

Hope it is doing something for you too as you read it.

Genuinely.

So, we HAVE to find a way of selling this communication thing and getting stuff done.

Easier said than done though.

And, just going back to the silo working thing again. It's really easy for people who work in safety to end up working in a silo if they're not careful and this goes back to the whole selling something that no-one wants to buy idea again, so you've got to watch that and work on this.

How to do it then?

You can achieve so much more by talking to people and working with them to find solutions, rather than sitting in the office wondering why people do or don't do stuff.

Note there then, that is talking TO people and not AT them.

Working WITH them and not AGAINST them.

Said it before and saying it again.

This is where you add value people, so really have a good go at getting this going.

In any team that I'm part of now I really encourage this, as I see it as probably one of the most important aspects of any team effort. Adding value by working with people and using communication skills to achieve this.

Written advice is important, and we've talked about the need for record keeping. But, also think about ways in which you can develop this. For example, like introducing an important report say, by actually talking to someone about the content first, or following up afterwards to see if your message has been understood.

Now, we all know that since the onset of the C-19 pandemic talking face to face took a bit of a back step, but don't let that go too far the other way and stop the talking.

We've all got used to using the online communication tools now and I know they're not the same, but we have to be resilient remember, adapt and keep moving forwards. So use what you have.

I was asked once what our "strategy" was in terms of safety, and I said this:

"Be present as much as possible".

What I meant was, not policing, but maintaining a constant "presence" over all of the company activities.

Knowing people and knowing what is really going on.

This means communicating with people.

All.

The.

Time.

I'm really lucky in my current team that I have highly motivated people who are both technically really good and also really, really, good people, people (the predictive grammar thing on the computer doesn't like people, people, but I do, so it's staying in).

What I'm saying is, that they've all seen a bit of what life can throw at you and they know the score. They communicate well and they're legit. Remember that bit?

And it's this that makes the being present thing work. Like, really work.

It all comes down to this in the end.

Communicating is THE most important thing we can do.

Don't make it complicated and try not to make it boring.

Sell it.

Don't tell it.

And "Talk To Me Goose".

"That's right Iceman. I am dangerous…"

Genius.

Chapter 6 - Don't Wait For Your Ship To Come In

So, this bit is all about making things happen for yourself, as it's an important part of the mind-set of what I'm trying to sell you. Call it self-motivation, determination or some other kind of positive sounding word ending with "tion".

The title "Don't Wait For Your Ship To Come In" is taken from a partial quote from Barry SHEEN, the totally awesome and fearless motorcycle rider and champion from the 70's and 80's. When I was young and kids actually played with toys rather than just video games, I had this little figure of him riding his motorbike. (Number 7 on his back of course).

Don't get me started on the X-Box and Play Station by the way, as it's a major issue currently. A friend of ours once told us giving a console to the kids was like "inviting a vampire into the house".

Great line.

If you've got kids and seen the movie "The Lost Boys", you'll perhaps understand...

"The Lost Boys".

The movie. Not the gang from "Peter Pan".

1987. The "BON JOVI" of vampire movies.

Kiefer SUTHERLAND. Jason PATRIC. The two Corey's – HAIM and FELDMAN. And "Bill" from "Bill and Ted".

Awesome film and soundtrack, which I had on cassette.

Watched every Halloween in our house as standard. Minus kids of course. Too young for it yet. For them it's, "Herbie Halloween", which, if unfamiliar, is a newish one with Adam SANDLER in it.

Pretty good actually.

"100% Fresh" is well worth a watch of his. He plays a mean guitar, you know. You should check it out. "Grown Ups" we've already discussed.

Anyway.

I had this figure of Barry SHEEN on his motorbike, and it was ace. I kept it for ages as well. My Grandad "gifted" it away one year to a local kids nursery, along with loads of other "Hot Wheels", that were like, "limited edition".

Gutted. I was twenty-five.

Point is, Barry SHEEN was cool and when he died, "Motorcycle News" did a piece with a great image of him riding his bike with his back to the camera. The quote above the image said,

"Don't Wait For Your Ship To Come In. Swim Out And Meet The Bloody Thing".

Words he had said and lived by. And those few words and the association I have to him have stayed with me a very long time.

Fun fact about Barry SHEEN then.

He ate a Mars bar every day.

Legend.

If you're after a bit of inspiration though, there it is right, there.

No, not eating a Mars bar every day. Even I know now that is a bad thing.

I'm talking about not sitting around waiting for things to happen for you.

If you sit around and expect things to come to you, they just won't.

You've got to get involved and make it happen. This might not be right away, and the path certainly isn't a straight line. And you'll probably have to zig zag to get to the destination as well.

But don't just sit there.

Go and get involved and make it happen for yourself.

Quick bit of advice then using a scenario from my old days.

I'll set the scene.

The blue lights and klaxons are on.

This is a 999 emergency.

A hurry up job, so getting to the scene pronto is important.

It's rush hour and there's loads of traffic.

The normal and shortest route to take to get there is to take the main road, but that's full of traffic.

So, you've got two choices:

Fight your way through and hope people oblige and pull over or out of the way (loads of people don't by the way, which I can semi-understand because some just don't like the rozzers because they lock you up, but to do it to the ambo and fire crews I just don't get)

Or

Turn the wheel and look for the sideways move that, whilst it may be a bit longer in terms of distance, stands you a better chance of actually getting you to where you need to be.

Zig zag to get there.

My advice?

Choose the second option.

This may seem an abstract idea or thought to some, which I totally get, so I'll try and give it some alternative context.

Career paths.

Very rare that these are ever a straight line, stretching back to choices made at school or college, even university, if you got that far.

Often, it's more a case of a path of opportunity that may present itself at any given time, or a situation that presents itself that is unplanned for.

Either way, in my experience there are not many people that have had a straight "path" and actually, I think it can really help to have done other things, as it builds up a "portfolio" of experience and a depth of understanding about wider issues.

Zig zag to get there.

It will make it more interesting and ultimately more rewarding.

And that's the thing to take-away.

The bit to think about.

It's never going to be straightforward.

But keep the objective in mind and work towards getting there. Be prepared to change direction, and even go back on yourself if it isn't working out, but make decisions and make them often.

Just don't sit still thinking things will work out without you doing something positive to make it happen.

"Swim out to the bloody thing".

Let's draw a parallel and try and add a bit more context then.

There's that tip of the iceberg diagram you may have seen that is used for different scenarios but, ultimately, it's saying kind of the same thing.

What you see at the tip of the iceberg hides underneath what is going on or has gone on.

I've just read that back and it needs a bit more explaining perhaps?

So, the diagram shows let's say, success or winning at the tip of the iceberg and that is the bit that most people see.

The much larger part though, that is hidden under the water, is all the hard work, failures and resilience, basically all the really hard stuff, commitment and effort it takes to get there.

It's a really good diagram that you should go and check out.

Note - I probably could insert a link or something here to it, but then that sort of defeats the object of getting out there and finding stuff out for yourselves, so off you go and do it on your own.

And if you've seen it already, or gone away and looked it up then it's a pretty decent way to visualise what I'm saying isn't it?

I think so. The point is.

Go and make it happen.

You'll get there if you want it enough.

"Don't wait for your ship to come in…"

Chapter 7 - Behind The Glitz and the Glamour

I'm giving you this bit because I thought it sort of went with the previous chapter on not waiting round for things to happen and the wider themes of being legit, investing in people and reflection.

Always be selling remember.

Note here then on a previous disclaimer.

I DID think the bit about awards and recognition adding value was a semi-good idea and so put it in here.

What I really want you to remember though, is that behind the showy, glitzy award stuff, is the REAL world.

Behind the awards and the recognition.

And the glitz and the glamour.

Is a load of hard and (often at times) gritty, unrelenting work.

Yes, you get a wear a virtual tuxedo or even a real one if you're lucky these days for an hour or two, or go to a posh do now and again, but the reality behind all that, is that getting there and probably more importantly for me, staying there, is all about hard work.

We've talked about some ideas on how to go about this and the importance of getting out there and being involved, so we're not going over all that again.

What we are doing now though is just having a little pause for thought, as it's about halfway through the book and I reckon a bit of "soak time" isn't a bad idea, so this is what I came up with.

I've done quite a lot of mentoring and work with younger people on employability, life skills and that sort of thing, and always try to work this idea in somewhere.

It's about not just thinking it's going to happen because you want it to or think it's deserved. Because that just doesn't happen. It's linked to the whole waiting for ships to come in and swimming out to them thing again.

I watched a documentary recently on Alex FERGUSON and his mindset.

Yes, the Man U manager.

Yes, this from a Liverpool fan.

Listen.

If there was a recent one on King Kenny or Jurgen then I'd use it here, but I couldn't see anything on Netflix or Amazon so you're getting FERGUSON alright?

The message is good though.

"Never give in".

Watch it.

The man talks a lot of sense.

In Scottish.

We could talk about how there's always light at the end of the tunnel, optimism and all that.

But for me, that doesn't quite do it.

You have to crawl through the tunnel to get to the light, so just keep going. And don't give in.

Said it before. I'm lucky.

Like proper lucky, in that I've worked in teams with motivated people who just get stuff done and I have people around me at home that are always there and remain positive.

Teamwork.

And that's what it is.

Team.

Work.

It is work.

It's what it takes to get results and stay positive.

There's some equations and quotations knocking about what you put in, you get out.

This IS the truth.

Mrs. J and I have 3 kids. And for us it is about the effort they put in, rather than the grades they get. If it's a case of A for effort. C for attainment. No problem. But the other way round, it's an issue.

Just a little something to pause on and soak up there then.

See what YOU think?

So, if you're winning and enjoying some success then hats off to you. You've put in the hard miles so enjoy going down the hill for a bit. But just for a bit, mind.

Because that's the other thing.

Never be satisfied.

Glitz and glamour is great but it fades.

The chase, the journey, whatever you want to call it, goes on forever.

Always be chasing.

Now then.

A quick message from me.

Thanks for getting this far with all this.

Joking aside, writing this has been a pretty big deal for me and to see it come together like this is brilliant, so thanks for being interested enough in the first place to pick it up and taking the time to have a read.

(Insert high five here. I will also accept a fist bump to show I am still hip and down with the kids).

Chapter 8 - Greed Is Good

"Greed is Good".

"Gordon GECKO" in the movie "Wall Street".

Which is a classic.

Massive phones, racket ball, power suits. The lot.

If you missed the 80's, it's got "Henry PIMM" from "Ant Man" in it, AKA Michael DOUGLAS. The second "Wall Street" movie we don't need to talk about. Movie sequels are never really as good the first.

Exceptions.

Of which there always are some:

"The Empire Strikes Back"

"Terminator 2"

"Aliens"

"The God Father Part 2"

"Toy Story 2"

Also, "Toy Story 3"

"Back To The Future 2" is a tricky one, because it is as good as the first one, not technically better, although it is better than the third one.

Feel free to discuss amongst yourselves.

Quick tale about the actual Wall Street in New York for you then from when Mrs. J and I went for my 40th birthday. Read into it what you will...

There is a big brass (I think it's made of brass) bull on Wall Street.

It was put there initially as a protest about capitalism, but it has since become an iconic bit of street art.

You are supposed to touch the big bull on its big old never nevers for luck.

Mrs. J was very interested in it.

Say no more. I as I say. Read into it what you wil...

Greed is good anyway.

What AM I talking about?

GG said famously or is it infamously?

Well, in the movie anyway he said, "Greed is good".

Now, on the face of it, yes, a full-on capitalist, money grabbing, negative kind of statement.

But, as I like to twist it up meanings and references every now and again and, given that I love a pop culture reference, I say this to you when putting it into context about learning, development and personal growth, greed is good.

Never be satisfied. Stay hungry and get greedy.

There is always something to be going after. Something to learn. Something to improve.

So be greedy and try and take in as much as you can.

I really encourage personal and professional development as I think it provides both the opportunity to learn and grow, as well as being a healthy distraction away from the day to day routine that keeps things fresh.

It just keeps it interesting.

It's just too easy to sit back and think that you've mastered something when the reality is that even when you're an "expert" at something, there will always be something else to learn.

CPD is a buzzword isn't it?

You know it.

Continual Professional Development.

Let's have a quick pretend debate.

Do you reckon people are born with natural talent and they just can do stuff?

Or

Can someone with a little natural talent work, nurture and develop skills, knowledge or ability, with a lot of dedication and hard work?

This is the point, if we were doing this for real, that we would sit around, perhaps in a horseshoe formation and discuss. So please, feel free to do so, if so inclined.

But, for the rest of us who haven't got the time or inclination for that then, I believe the answer is probably somewhere in between both ideas.

It definitely helps to have some natural ability. I would say that really helps.

Daughter Number 1 and Brother Number 2 both have natural ability with a football.

But both have had to also really work at developing it too. And they have both been greedy in their pursuit of this. Training. Fitness. Diet. Matches. Dedication.

A brilliant effort and I'm very proud of them both.

Far too much running for me like. I'm happy being the taxi service.

But they both keep at it and are very good at it.

Properly good.

Got my hopes on Daughter Number 1 one day pulling on the England shirt.

Never give in.

A "greedy" mind set can really help as well though when it comes to developing competence.

You know, the knowledge, skills, abilities and experience thing.

Being a trusted advisor to an organisation has immense value and is something we definitely need to have a focus on. This comes via investing in yourself, learning stuff and then putting it into practice.

I have always wanted to be the "safe pair of hands" or "go to person" for information and solutions as, frankly makes me feel good and I like having that reputation. This just doesn't happen because I want it to though. It takes time and work to create it and to keep it going.

You can become outdated really fast.

Especially now we have the Internet, social media and all the other digital advancements that make that phone you bought yesterday, obsolete by tomorrow.

A quick tale from the student days then.

I went to Leeds University in the late '90's.

No internet.

Someone in the library (it was next to the Student Union bar) used to talk about the "Information Highway" and showed it to me once on a computer screen but I thought,

"This thing will never catch on. Too complicated".

(You can see why I never got that job in Silicon Valley…)

Anyway, in the first year of university you had to pick extra subjects called electives to study alongside your main degree. I picked film studies (naturally) and this thing called "Coding", as it was near the top of the list that was in alphabetical order, and I wasn't really paying attention.

Loved the film study.

Hated the Coding.

It was all maths, and this stuff called an algorithm, which I had never heard of (probably because I am pretty rubbish at Maths and somehow just scraped a B grade at GCSE).

I couldn't get the algorithm to make a picture of the Union Jack flag (that was the assignment) at the end of the course and I failed it.

Fast forward twenty-something years and they teach Coding at Primary School now. Algorithms are what social media uses to make us buy stuff. And without the Internet, none of us would be doing anything anymore. Including reading this...

Amazing.

My kids understand it all.

I still can't make a picture of the Union Jack.

Dinosaur.

Greed is good anyway. So, get learning.

Don't think though that this means you don't share any of this because this is definitely not what we're about.

Yes, we want to be the best that we can be at what we do and are hungry for ideas and knowledge. But the idea then, is to share this with those that are around and add value by developing other people to have this same kind of mind-set.

The more people know and understand the better they can perform.

Pretty straightforward.

Another true tale.

"Knowledge is power".

I had a really dodgy T-shirt when I was about 13 with this phrase on and a picture of "Reg HOLDSWORTH" from "Coronation Street" on.

Don't really know why I bought it, as I am not a fan.

I think it was because Morrissey was.

HMV (my favourite shop growing up) had some great T-Shirts.

I bought my Dad one once with a picture of "Victor MELDREW" from TV show "One Foot In The Grave "on the front.

On the back it said, "You Miserable Bastard".

He wore it once to one of my parent's evenings.

Genius.

I am really keen on mentoring and try to support as many people as I can.

There are some really good platforms available now that make it much easier for people to reach out and I encourage people to look at these, as it can really help to speak to someone rather than slogging away at something and getting frustrated or deflated if the result doesn't come.

I think the safety community is pretty good at this. So, if you're not up on this yet, check it out and get involved.

When you get into the mentoring or coaching thing proper you can come away learning as much as from the person you are supporting as they can from you.

Truth right there.

And, you may find (as I do) that it sort of feels good and then you want more and more of it.
Hey, I'm no chemist or biology expert. But it's something about endorphins or something...

GCSE science grade B was it for me so I'm probably way off with that but, whatever it is, it's a good thing.

You will notice here then it was also a grade B in science as well as maths for me.

Neither were my thing.

English however was - A*

Perhaps, I should have done something with it earlier. Instead, I went on to university to read History (also grade B) much to Dad's dismay.

What can I say?

I have to do things my own way. And we're here now.

(And yes, Dad you're right for my tenth birthday I should have got the mountain bike that time instead of the racer, but I wanted to be Barry SHEEN and hang over the bike with the drop handlebars, OK?)

Conclusion

(Like in a grade B science experiment).

Greed is good.

Stay hungry.

Never be satisfied.

Keep wanting to learn, develop, grow and then ultimately give something back.

And if you're under 25 and wondering…

HMV was a shop.

A real shop.

It sold records, CDs, videos, DVDs and T-shirts and other cool stuff.

Ask   your   parents.

Chapter 9 - 2 Magnums And A Calypso

We've talked a lot about getting people on board with you and using all the tools available to sell your ideas and essentially, get people to buy into what you're trying to sell.

However, there may be time when an opportunity arises that it may be as beneficial for YOU to buy into THEM. This is equally an important thing to recognise and one that shows both your appreciation of people and just leaves them with that warm fuzzy feeling that only chocolate or ice cream can bring.

True Story Time Number 1

When I was a young police officer, I got the opportunity to move into one of the highly sought after specialist units. This was brilliant and where frankly, I found out who I was and basically grew up. I really idolised my Sergeant at the time and the guys I worked with.

It was an action-packed and very exciting time in my life.

There were many, many adventures, both in and out of work.

There were good times. Some great times. And some sad times. Working very closely with people for a long time and in this type of high pressurised, high risk, environment creates a sort of weird "family".

I'd be lying if I said I didn't miss many aspects of that kind of working life. Everyone was encouraged and expected to be a leader and I looked up to, and respected a lot of people, both senior to me in rank and within my own peer group.

However, one of the standout leadership moments is so basic, and so throw away, but at the same time, so effective (or is at affective?), that it has stayed with me 15 years later.

And it was the simple act of pulling into a garage on nights in the van and the Sergeant going inside and coming out with a Crunchie for each of us.

I know.

This seems like nothing.

And in the grand scheme of things. It was NOTHING. Not really. I don't doubt it was just intended as a nice gesture at the time and nothing more.

But why then have I remembered it and thought enough of it to tell you about it now?

This was during a proper macho culture time in my life by the way. No mental health awareness. Not much safety awareness if I'm honest. Some tough people doing some dangerous work at times and putting themselves in harms way and at risk and then relying on a joke and a smile to normalise.

This seemingly random act of kindness though broke through all of that and spoke volumes, to me at least.

Weird.

But why?

Because it IS the little things that can make a difference to people. So be kind and give a shit.

Never neglect this bit.

A smile.

A hello.

Knowing and remembering someone's name is a brilliant way to help you build a relationship with people by the way.

And chocolate does no harm either.

Chocolate is ace full stop.

Perhaps it's because a Crunchie is my all-time favourite choccy bar that it had the impact it did.

Who knows?

Quick debate.

What is the best and worst chocolate bar?

The best I say is a Crunchie.

However, coming a close second is the red Lindor's that melt in your mouth.

These are for special occasions in our house. Birthdays and Christmas.

Mrs. J likes a Ferrero Roche.

Fancy.

She also digs a Chocolate Orange and a Mint Aero.

Both of which are just wrong, along with any other fruit-based chocolate.

Luckily for me then the kids like them, so a box of Quality Street or something similar, lasts about five minutes in our house.

The top of the wrong chocolate tree of course though, has to be Turkish Delight.

Roses and chocolate separate.

Fine.

The "taste" of roses mixed in with a chocolate bar?

Evil.

Debate amongst yourselves at your leisure.

True Story Time Number 2

Joking aside, recognition is a big thing, and you should look to do it as often as you can.

In one of my units, we had a Chief Inspector who had a bit of a fierce reputation and was someone who, for the rank and file, you only really spoke to if you were in trouble for something. This kind of leadership style is not uncommon in uniformed, disciplined service and sort of goes with the territory.

What he was good at though, was using a little tool of a recognition letter or a memo, whenever there was a job well done. This again worked for me as it gave a similar feeling of a chocolate bar, granted not as good, but you can't keep having chocolate bars all the time or you'll end up the size of a house.

It served to let you know though that he knew what the team(s) were doing and that this work was acknowledged.

This is a GOOD THING and one I've unashamedly taken with me everywhere else since.

I currently call these "Good Call" letters and issue them to people when they make a good call in terms of safety. This idea has also developed on the people engagement side with our friends in HR, in the form of "Going the Extra Mile" recognition.

Small things I know, but ones that make a difference and make people feel recognised and part of something.

The staff letters approach can also be used as an awareness piece, and this also works when things don't quite go to plan or again people do the whole crazy shit thing.

But be sure to have balance though.

There is a time and a place for the old carrot and stick approach. But use both.

True Story Time Number 3

People remember things.

Often small things. Really don't under-estimate that.

Not long into my tenure with a new company I was out and about starting to sell the safety message. There was a lot of work to do, and this was right at the start of the journey. It's well-known in the construction sector about the risks involved with working at height, so I would pick out jobs involving this kind of risk and focus on those, as this was clearly a big issue and one that we needed to get right.

I had joined in the summer, so the weather was pretty good and warm. I went out to see some people who were doing some work on a flat roof at the back of a petrol forecourt. The works manager and I had already had some conversations about edge protection and working with fall arrest equipment and it was good to see when I got there, that this was in hand.

I spoke before about knowing when to move and act. You have to be able to recognise and take advantage of opportunity whenever it presents itself.

And this was one such opportunity.

To sell the message and get buy in.

To make people feel valued for their contribution and recognise the right behaviours.

We're dipping our toe into human factors and behavioural safety here people, so listen up.

The approach?

Buying two Magnums and a Calypso from the forecourt shop as a treat for a bit of good, safe work.

The cost?

Less than a fiver. The Magnums were on offer.

The result?

Three, happy smiling faces sat off enjoying a little victory that is eating an ice cream in the sun.

The real result?

Safety message sold, bought and remembered. Like forever. And I say this because when they see me, they always ask me if I'm going to the shop for an ice cream. And they're always working safely.

Now, I'm not saying to you go out now and buy everyone an ice cream or a chocolate bar and all will be well, because that just isn't true.

But, recognising people will never do you any harm and helps build relationships that have meaning and that really helps to sell ideas.

Powerful, but simple stuff.

And they were Almond Magnums by the way. Hands down the best.

Chapter 10 - Defences In Depth and Big Risks

We've talked quite a bit so far then about style and approach I suppose and how to go about selling the idea of safety. So, I thought it would also be a good idea to offer you just a few pointers on some practical bits to go with all this then. Some things that have helped me along the way and that I use in the day to day.

This bit is about risk management, and we'll also look at investigations and the value behind near misses in the next couple of chapters.

Earlier on in the book then, I said my piece about the "HEINRICH Triangle" and shared my thoughts on it.

Completely my opinion and leaving it there.

You may agree. You may not. Entirely up to you.

There are lots of theories and models out there and some of them are really good and I get, and some others are either far too complicated for my brain to understand or, just don't light that spark of an idea that speaks directly to me.

One that does though, and did straight away, was the whole "Swiss Cheese" model thing.

I told you earlier we were going to have a chat about it at some point and this then seems like the right time.

Bit of background then if you need it, and I MEAN just a bit. Go and look at this more in your own time if you need to. It is good, and will be worth the effort.

The "Swiss Cheese" model belongs to James REASON. It is a way of visualising risk and creating barriers or "defences in depth" to try and stop "risk" passing through. It recognises that whatever barriers or defences you put in place, these will have some holes in them (I will explain this in a minute with some examples) and that the idea is, that you try and prevent the holes from lining up, so that the "risk" manages to come through and become fully realised.

Note to self whilst typing.

A diagram showing this also would be good here. If this ever sees the light of day get someone to put one in.

Further note and reality at the time of publishing and final proof reading.

This is too hard to do. Tell them to go and find this stuff out for themselves. Greed is good and all that, blah blah blah...

So, let's try and put some real-life perspective on this then, so that we can use it and bring it to life as a proper strategy. (Get the diagram, it will help)

See? You might actually learn something after all.

Let's pick a risk.

I'll stick with the ideas I've used before about "Big Risks" and pick some construction sector risks. This one is about work at height, because as we all know, this is a major issue.

So how do we go about using the "Swiss Cheese" model to map our approach the managing this risk?

Here's how I would do it.

Think of each "slice" of "Swiss Cheese" as one of your controls.

These could be risk assessments, training, competence, awareness, edge protection, fall arrest systems, equipment checks or PPE for example.

Line them up "slice by slice" and they create a "defence" against the risk created by working at height i.e., someone or something falling.

This is the idea of creating "defences in depth".

Now in each defence there could be "holes".

(Like in a piece of Swiss Cheese. I was going to go off on one here again and discuss real cheese, but this is important and we're doing well so let's concentrate now).

These holes could come from a risk assessment that isn't as good as it should be. Let's use some proper terminology here for a moment then – "suitable and sufficient". Or, it could be training that has expired perhaps or isn't followed, awareness that isn't quite there or complacency has set in, edge protection that isn't right or PPE that is damaged or not suitable for the task.

The list is endless.

What you have to constantly keep doing then, is recognising this, and filling or moving the holes around so that the risk doesn't come through and reach the end of the defences. It's when all the holes in the defences line up that the risk is fully realised, and you get an outcome.

So fill the holes by doing a decent risk assessment in the first place. Keep training up to date and current. Keep awareness going. Keep it interesting and look for new ways to sell it. Keep edge protection issues in check through competence and site inspections. Consistency remember, is the key. And the same goes for equipment checks and PPE. Go back to basics and check, check, check.

Doing it this way and using the model to visualise the strategy can help to explain why we are going about things in this way. It can help to sell the idea without boring people with stacks of legislation and switching them off.

Let's pick another one of our "Big Risks" and apply the model again.

Asbestos.

Big risk.

A lot has been done on this, both in terms of training, education and procedures, and rightfully so, but there is still a really long way to go with this one.

Side note (serious).

There are loads of free resources available to help with this. If this is a risk in your workplace, then you really have got to get to grips with it.

Asbestos is not like an injury that would come from a fall from height, where the outcome is instant and very clear to see. It is much more dangerous in a way, because it is a latent issue and the "outcome" is sitting there, developing in the lungs, latent for many years, doing its damage and only becomes clear once it is too late.

Lecture over. You know what to do.

Swiss cheese and asbestos then.

Line up your defences in depth.

Here we go.

Training.

And proper training that is applicable to the right level of work that is being done. This is where knowing your stuff comes in people. Read the Regs and interpret them properly.

Surveys and samples. Understand the need for a survey and the right kind before any work is done. Again, know your stuff. Add your value.

Emergency procedures.

Have some, because there may come a time when the first two defences aren't enough.

Line them up.

Keep the holes moving around and manage the risk before the holes line up and the risk makes it through.

I could go on and on with this, but I hope this helps to get my point across and sell it to you, so that you can think about how to pass this on and sell it further down the line.

I've used this idea a lot and it seems to work and fits in with the whole Safety Salesman approach.

I saw it used to explain the response to C-19, which is good because it shows it is still a valid model and for me, it worked as a visual. Again, if you're interested, go and find out about it.

If you think about things like the lockdowns, social distancing, awareness (the whole hands, face, space thing), test and trace and the vaccination programme, then these are all defences, built up in depth to try and prevent the risk from coming through or at least manage it with some kind of structure.

It works.

Think about using it as a risk management tool.

Key points then.

Recognise your risk(s).

Build your defences in depth.

Keep the defences moving.

Makes sense to me James REASON.

Sold.

I'll buy it.

Chapter 11 - The Golden Hour

Practical bit part two then.

Investigating.

Not really taught in my opinion in the mainstream qualifications, albeit there are some new courses coming out that look OK.

Yes, we get the 5 whys thing or a fish bone root cause diagram, but this never really spoke to me when I looked at it.

Now remember, I'm coming at this from being in the cops, where investigating stuff is a pretty big deal and the training you get, especially in the CID, is top drawer. I'd spent just under 10 years in uniform before I dipped my toe into investigations proper, so I was pretty well versed in procedure, but the investigators course was next level.

Easily the best course I ever went on.

At the time I did it in 2009-2010, you did a Foundation Degree in Criminal Investigation as part of the course via the University of Central Lancashire, so you came out with a decent qualification at the end too. Point is, I reckon this is one of my top skills and I am going to share with you some top tips, so pay attention...

The Golden Hour.

This relates to the time just after an incident, when gathering evidence is most vital. It's not really an hour, but I suppose it makes it sound important by giving it a time stamp and calling it "golden".

What is important to understand though, is that evidence can disappear quickly, so you do need to move pretty sharpish to try and capture it.

Having a structure to the investigation will help this and we'll look at this and some big, broad lines of enquiry in a minute.

What it does mean though is that you have to get up, leave the air-conditioned office and go to the scene. If you are thinking of doing this desktop stuff and don't put "eyes on" a scene, then you are just doing it wrong.

Stop it.

Get your bag, a pen and something to write on if you are old skool, or a phone/tablet if you're under forty, also something that you can take photos with and another thing to measure with (a ruler or tape measure is a good idea) and get out there.

To assist in bringing this to life a bit here then, let's imagine we've had an accident on a busy site where someone has fallen from height. They are injured and have been taken to hospital. You've been told about it just after it happened and are on the way to the site.

(Yes, in reality this may very well attract Regulatory attention, but getting involved and being proactive can and will be seen in a positive light).

Got an image of the scenario in your mind?

Good.

Let's look at some lines of enquiry then.

Before we do that though, remember to use open questions.

More on these in the next chapter, but quickly for now so this bit makes sense, these questions start with:

WHO, WHAT, WHY, WHERE, WHEN and HOW?

Firstly then, place/scene enquiries. Ask questions and start recording things like:

WHAT and HOW it happened? Get the circumstances.

WHEN did it happen? Start a timeline.

WHERE did it happen? Get the location and go to it. Photos. Preserve the scene and prevent access.

WHO was involved? Get their details. Statements.

WHAT work was going on at the time and WHY it was being done? Think RAMS.

Secondly, people related enquiries then. So, what have we got?

The injured party.

WHO are they? Full details – name, address, date of birth, next of kin, training certificates if relevant and available.

WHAT are the injuries? Statements, photos.

WHO are the witnesses? Are they any? Is there any CCTV?

Third line of enquiry. Equipment, materials – think things like plant, machinery, vehicles. This is a work at height incident in our scenario, so maybe there was scaffolding involved or a piece of access equipment that maybe of interest.

Again, big open questions.

WHAT equipment was involved?

WHERE is it now?

WHAT records does it have? Start collecting information. Photos.

It is unusual in safety related investigations to have forensics as a line of enquiry, so we'll not go there, but do think about preserving scenes, equipment and not moving it – especially if the incident is likely to attract regulatory attention. Take photos. Measurements help as well sometimes. In this scenario think HOW far was the fall or HOW wide was the gap maybe?

The point of all of this is to search for the truth.

Gather as much evidence as you can in the "Golden Hour."

Fact.

Most crimes are solved in the first 72 hours after they happen. After that, it gets harder and harder to find and preserve the evidence. Time really is the enemy of an effective investigation, so move quickly.

If you start to think about the investigation process like this, then you'll stand a decent chance of doing a comprehensive job that looks professional and then can be used for some of the other good stuff like preventing it happening again perhaps.

Being able to do an effective investigation, as I have found out, is a VERY transferrable skill across many other disciplines like HR and general management, so try and practice it as often as you can.

I could spend a lot longer on this and sitting here now writing, I'm thinking this is probably a whole thing on its own that I need to think about doing as a separate piece.

There are things to tell you about how to put the evidence together into a report to present to others such as management, the insurer or even the regulator and how that can really add value. And maybe this could go with how to interview people properly using the PEACE model as well.

I'll have a think and if I come up with anything good you'll be the first to know.

Investigations skills are really valuable and can help to sell the idea of getting safety right and add real value, so take a bit of time to consider whether this is something that you could improve on or develop.

But I'll stop there for now.

Remember, big open questions and think about structuring your lines of enquiry.

That is all.

End of lesson.

Chapter 12 - Good Calls And The Value Of A Near Miss

Now, there's lots of debate on whether a near miss is a leading indicator or a lagging indicator, and if you look on any of the MANY forums there are in this game, you'll find lots of people saying their bit on this topic.

And a lot of hot air too.

Does it really matter?

Not really.

What DOES matter though to me, is two things.

Firstly.

That leading AND lagging indicators (that add value) are a good thing. It's pretty much received and established wisdom that looking at both is a good idea.

Secondly.

Near misses DO have value and they can be used as a preventative tool, as a learning tool and as a recognition tool.

Come with me now friends and let's discuss.

Prevention.

So, let's look at a near miss scenario then.

We'll say something connected with work at height that came about as a result of a site visit you were doing (as you're now really proactive and getting out there and seeing what's really going on).

We know by now don't we, the value of site visits and getting out there and finding out what is really going on?

So it's natural AND probable that when you operate like this, you are going to start to uncover these types of things more.

It was a near miss then, because it was not fully realised and there was not an adverse outcome, like an injury or damage. But there WAS every opportunity or potential.

Classic definition of a near miss, yes?

This near miss has REAL value then, if it is shared and used, not so much as a leading or lagging indicator, but as a POSITIVE indicator to prevent it happening again.

Carrot AND stick time.

There are some people out there who say you can have either one or the other. But I don't really agree with this, and believe that both are valid options.

I do absolutely agree that "carrot" should come first, but there are times, given investigation or circumstance, that "stick" should be considered. This is the notion of "fair blame", and that again is very well discussed in most safety qualifications and training, so I'm not going to go into it in loads of detail here.

All I'm saying is, that there are on occasion, times when invoking discipline procedures are the right option and are a valid tool in preventing incidents.

Now, I appreciate that this may be the policeman in me racing to the surface, but whatever it is, it's important to understand when to move and when to sit still remember. If, after proper investigation we find ourselves in violation territory, then for me, that's where we are.

Act accordingly and come to your own conclusions.

It isn't a bed of roses out there in the real world and you'll need to have a pretty thick skin in this game. Make the call and be prepared to back it up.

This IS a fact.

You already know this.

I really do hope that from reading this you're picking up some tips and ideas on how to go about it and sell the message. Don't think though that from time to time you may have to upset a few folk though.

Our friends in HR of course can support us with this, when the time comes...

So have a little think about using a near miss as a prevention tool.

It's very valid and doing this has a lot of value.

Next then.

Using them for learning.

A near miss can be a great way to learn. This is why they are a positive thing.

Sticking with the same near miss scenario then involving work at height, we can ask about what went wrong or how it came about, or what step in a process was missed?

Notice anything about any of those questions by the way?

Correct.

These are all our big, OPEN questions.

5WH anybody?

I actually learnt 5WH long before I was in the CID and actually got taught it in GCSE English – (A* as you know).

"Open" questions people.

WHAT?

WHERE?

WHEN?

WHO?

WHY?

And

HOW?

It's thirty years now since I was at school.

Isn't it funny how some things stay with you from school that are actually really useful?

It's also funny how some absolutely useless stuff just stays with you as well though.

Example.

I remember from Year 9 German how to ask, "Do you have a budgie?" and answer back "No. But I do have a small mouse".

Yet I couldn't ask for basic directions when I was in Berlin once or even order a beer properly.

Go figure.

But asking these kind of questions (the open questions, not the budgie one, forget about the budgie) can help to drive responses that may provide some useful answers and opportunity to learn.

That can only be a good and positive thing.

Lastly then.

Recognition and specifically recognising a good call.

Really don't underestimate the value and impact that recognising people can have. Especially when it comes to something like reporting stopping work because conditions were unsafe, or something wasn't right.

Dynamic risk assessment anyone?

It takes confidence to call things out when they are not right and if you're working in a place where this might be a new idea, then stick with it as it takes a bit of time for people to feel confident in coming forward.

Seriously.

If you're not already doing this then start. Like now.

Making a good call to stop work should get recognised every time.

This could be in a letter, a bulletin, an email or a simple verbal acknowledgement.

Whatever form it takes, just make sure it gets done.

Making it an official thing, like a letter I really like. And also let other people know about it too.

You're acknowledging people for doing the RIGHT thing here, so sharing it will help to raise awareness and (hopefully) give other people some assurance that they're not going to be had off for reporting something like a near miss, which let's face it, still can have negative connotations attached to them.

Ultimately, it's about taking positive action that makes a difference and adds that all important value.

Learn. Prevent. Recognise.

Class dismissed.

Chapter 13 - Stealth and Safety

So right from the get-go this title belongs to Daughter Number 1 (who is at the time of writing this 11). We were sat talking about what it was I did for a job one evening and I think she was sounding me out to see if it was interesting enough to bring me into school for the whole "parents explain their jobs to the kid's" day. She was convinced I did "Stealth and Safety" and this made me laugh.

When I started writing I began to write ideas or things that sounded interesting to me down so that I could remember and use them later.

And in this modern age this means typing them into my phone (because at home at least, I can never find a pen) and "Stealth and Safety" went straight into the notes section. I had no real idea what it was going to mean at that point, but I just loved it.

So, this bit has come from the title phrase first and then had the idea built around it, but I think it works and fits in with everything that we have been talking about, so let's get into it.

We'll go back then first, to the idea at the start of the book, that this safety business can be about selling something that most people don't want to buy or think that they don't to buy.

This is a very real issue and one that I think we just have to accept.

There are loads of other things going on that make what we're selling either unattractive or just not as attention grabbing as it should be.

I know, everyone talks about "safety first" blah blah blah, but how many REALLY mean it?

We are up against it here people, so we have to recognise this fact first and then think about some ways in which we can go about our business and "sell" the idea of good safety.

We've talked loads already about some ways of doing this and I hope there are some genuine take-aways (in-between the abstract music and film trivia and tales from my youth).

The idea of "Stealth and Safety" is another one that I hope you get and start to use then.

It goes something like this.

So, we know that quoting loads of legislation and threats of prison for the big boss don't really go over that well and neither does the clipboard totting and tutting safety plod, who just tells everyone off and says no all the time.

We do know that we have to be engaging, collaborative, supportive and solutions driven to add real value that gets results. Right?

It's a lovely sentiment that, and one, if it were that easy to do and achieve, it wouldn't need any more explaining.

Which MEANS it isn't that easy.

In fact, it's REALLY hard.

But we are up for it and know that, achieving our goals is not a straight line and that we have to zig zag to get there.

A bit of a recap to see if you have been paying any attention then...

So, you have the blue lights and sirens on.

It's rush hour (It always is by the way, when these jobs come out. That, or in the middle of the night when you are done in and it's just about time for changeover).

The quickest way to get to where you need to be is of course is that lovely straight road. But there is traffic everywhere.

All the lights are on red.

And now there is a herd of cows crossing up ahead.

Side Note.

(There never once was a herd of cows crossing on the streets of Merseyside but there was once a Rhino on a roundabout. A tale for another time).

Stay with me.

Do you?

Try and fight your way through, taking the straight line?

Or?

Turn the wheel and take the long way around, which in the end may cost that little bit extra in fuel or be a bit further to travel, but ultimately will get you there faster?

If your answer was the first option then close this book. Go and get that clipboard and the high viz vest and start telling people "No".

But my friends, if you chose the second option and I know that you did, then congratulations you're getting somewhere. Because it isn't about always taking the straight road that is right in front of you.

Sometimes we have to duck and weave to achieve.

I literally just thought of that phrase as I wrote it.

"Duck and weave to achieve". Trademarked. Patent pending. It's mine. You can't have it.

That is the first thing to understand.

The second, is that getting there doesn't have to be a big loud deal that draws loads of attention, as this can create alienation and a silo.

We never want to work in a silo.

To achieve this then involves a bit of stealth.

Here is a definition of "stealth" I've taken from a real English dictionary.

"Doing something quietly and carefully so no-one will notice what you are doing..."

We can work with this idea people.

The idea of safety doesn't have to be in your face or even directly reference safety at all.

Oh, the shock. The horror.

Remember, we are about adding value and finding solutions.

We are interested in building relationships with people and working with them and not against them. We want to invest in people and be seen as the go to people for others.

I believe that really effective people in this game, come to realise that, they are in fact a bit commercial, a bit HR, a bit operational.

In fact, they are a bit of everything and that is why it is a really interesting and challenging thing to be part of and doing.

And using a bit of stealth, so that "no-one will notice what you are doing", can in fact be a really effective way of selling this message.

Keep doing it and this is how you build culture.

This high idea of "this is how we do things around here".

It doesn't happen overnight, and it really needs work, buy-in and consistency. But stick with it.

The road to get there will certainly not be a straight line.

Sometimes you will hit a dead end and need to make a U-turn.

Sometimes you will need to change direction altogether.

This is normal.

Sometimes your work will be very overt and very clear to see.

But at other times, it will all be about what is going on behind the scenes and in the background.

And by having little, discreet conversations that, outwardly bear no connection to safety at all with people, it can be these that in the long term, can have a very definite and long-lasting effect on it.

Daughter Number 1 was right.

From the mouths of babes, ladies and gentlemen.

"Stealth and Safety".

Chapter 14 - Less Is More

OK, so this chapter is about keeping things concise, to the point and simple. The list of legislation in this game is literally endless. There are codes of practice, guidance notes, standards, management systems, certifications, accreditations, assessments. All that.

Not saying that they're not important, but come on.

Wouldn't it be easier if there were just maybe, a little less...words?

I've thought on this for a good while throughout writing this book.

I've even gone so far as to research things like,

"How many words should a non-fiction book have?"

Or

"How many pages should a factual book should have?"

And then in the end, it sort of just came to me that this way of thinking was completely against the whole Safety Salesman/Shoot From The Lip thing. I was looking at what other people had done in terms of how many pages or words they'd written and had a misbelief that this was what my thing should look like. Like this in someway would validate it.

Wrong.

In the end, it shouldn't be about how many words or pages there are. It just needs to be enough to get the point across and more importantly, understood doesn't it?

I also got some really great advice to "Tell MY truth" when it came to writing and I wrote this down straight away when I heard it (I had an emergency pen in my jacket pocket). And this gave me the final piece in the jigsaw that really did validate it all for me. This was and is what I have to say, so I'm just saying it how I see it.

Shoot From The Lip. (My truth. Thanks Karen).

There are loads of people out there, again with some proper long funny letters after their names, that probably know chapter and verse of every bit of law or whatever, but can they actually TALK to people and get people to LISTEN and UNDERSTAND?

Maybe it's just me, but I've met quite a few people that turn me off when they talk and I'm at least semi-interested in the subject, so what chance do they have with the rest of the folk out there?

Less IS More I say.

Real life tale coming up.

So, when I first started out in the safety game I had some good knowledge, some qualifications and I'd say a half decent idea about life in general, but when it came to writing things like business proposals and asking people for money for projects, I hadn't got a great deal of experience.

Policing wasn't really like that. The set up was well established and my roles at least, were pretty much mapped out. If you needed equipment or gear to do a job, you went and saw the equipment officer and (within reason) you got it.

Further note of experience here to pass if at all relevant.

The equipment officer is well worth getting to know if you ever find yourself in any kind of organisation that operates with one.

Consider flattery, buying lunch and even giving small gifts if necessary. As, once you get granted access to the "Aladdin's Cave" that is the stores, you will quickly learn why some people have all the best gear and you are still rocking those boots with the hole in them or someone else's smelly overalls.

Basic stuff, but an essential life experience lesson I thought I'd share.

We were talking business proposals.

And for these to be effective it is about getting your point or proposal across on no more than one side of A4.

This was the advice I got from my then boss, in one of my first post-police roles and I've used it ever since and it works.

It was his thing that, if you couldn't sell your idea in a page then you didn't know your stuff well enough, so how would anyone else be expected to know it and therefore understand it either?

Now, there may be some well-read types here that have heard all this before, and I agree that this is not a new idea, but it was the first time I was hearing it, so he gets the credit from me OK?

And this actually WORKS by the way. And here's an example.

One of my first proposals (and one which was both successful and one that I am pretty proud of achieving) was to have defibrillators installed. This was 2015 and I was working for the local College.

I knew it was a good idea and there was plenty of support for it. But being the public sector, money was tight, so I had to come up with something other than "This is a good idea so buy them", that would get the senior team's attention and provide a solution that made sense.

And this is what a lot of this is about.

You have to learn the "management speak" a bit and understand what motivates the money holders and the decision makers.

This IS the sell.

Quoting laws, regulations and stats doesn't get the job done.

We have to be better than that.

So, what I did with this one was to look at some ways that this idea could be funded first.

Being a first aider at the College carried a small bonus payment and there were literally loads of people who were identified as being first aiders. However, when I looked at who actually ever did any first aid, it was clear that there was a pattern of people who were regularly used. And it was these people who put their training to good use and were the right people for this very important role.

So, by having an understanding of the relevant legislation and law on first aider numbers first and then doing a little risk assessment, I was able to produce a one pager that both reduced the College pay out for first aiders who were never used and put forward an idea that would more than pay for the defies.

Simple. But effective.

Fast forward a couple of months, as these things do take a little time, and we installed four cabinets in the reception areas of each campus, each with a brand new defib in.

Result.

I even did a little deal with the company I bought them from (always look for deals by the way, there are loads to be done) to get a training module included, which was then used by the College First Aid Trainer (who was brilliant by the way). She also gave me some great input on which ones to buy, so it was even more of a win, as it was a proper partnership approach.

It was presented as a simple proposal that had a start, a middle and an end. It identified the problem and found the solution, including costs and savings.

No reams of paper.

No quoting laws.

No empty coercion that someone might go to jail if we didn't do it.

Just an idea that this was the right thing to do, presented in a way people could understand and follow, with the proposed outcome justified.

One page. Job done.

This doesn't just apply to getting money out of people either though to fund projects or ideas.

There are other things I say keep simple.

Let's talk risks for a minute then. And more precisely risk assessments and risk management.

So, I totally get it that legislation tells us that we need suitable and sufficient risk assessments for the stuff that we do in work.

No breaking news there.

However, there is this tendency to try and cover absolutely everything that could possibly EVER happen.

EVERY possible scenario.

Like EVER.

What IF this or that happens?

What IF?

What IF?

This is impossible to assess and frankly a waste of time and paper.

Instead, I say to you concentrate on the "big risks". Be realistic and be sensible.

Less IS more.

To do this you have to get your risk profile right first of course.

Understand what you're working with and where the real risk is and focus on that.

I've talked a lot about "Big Risks" before and as you know, I currently work in the construction sector. You don't have to be Sherlock Holmes to work out that falls from height are a major issue. Work at height in general is, so for me that definitely needs loads of attention.

Asbestos is another big risk and again, there are no prizes for knowing a bit about how dangerous this stuff is, as there is loads of (free) info out there. So again, for me, this is a key area to focus on, getting out there and educating people and getting processes right.

But the real value for me with this risk based approach came with another identified "big risk".

So, I currently work in the construction sector right and a large part of the work involves reactive maintenance. And this means lots of people driving around the UK fixing stuff.

And that is just it.

Driving.

When I looked at the activities the people did the most, and used some good data to back this up, the task they actually spent most of the day doing wasn't construction related at all.

It was driving for work.

This could, and in fact had, been previously overlooked, as a very significant risk.

To tackle this then, I went back to basics.

Remember, we're not re-inventing the wheel here.

Deliberate driving related pun there. Funny me.

Do a risk assessment.

And for driving for work you know it's the whole driver, vehicle and journey thing.

Look at your risk for each and then think about what controls you need.

My team ended up putting loads of stuff in place including going proactive with the vehicle inspections using digital templates, setting up a partnership programme with a well-known training provider for some really good driver training, doing e-risk assessments for each driver that enabled us to properly understand our risk profile and educating people on journey planning too.

Nothing really fancy though.

Just good, solid risk management in my opinion.

The result?

Less accidents, which of course is great.

But also, further down the line, reductions in insurance premiums, which is always good as the "money" in any organisation always appreciates this. And, if you're really clever here and build up a good relationship, you can start to then look at ways in which these savings can be re-invested for other programmes or ideas that continue the improvement piece.

Also though, as the results started to come in year on year, recognition also started to come in from industry players, magazine article pieces and award wins.

All of which are priceless PR.

You know, the commercial stuff we have to become part of to add value and help our cause and message.

Less IS more.

Remember, there are no prizes for using the most words and certainly no one is really interested in how much you know, if they can't understand you or the message you're trying to get over.

Complicated plans, proposals and ideas are really hard to maintain and sustain whenever there are humans involved and remember sometimes, as we know, people just do some crazy shit. (Nan really won't be happy with this, as I've used it a fair few times now. I can feel the stern look, but it's staying in. I'll buy two cakes).

So go then my friends and do your level best to keep things simple.

I know. I know. It's hard.

But the real trick here is to know your stuff well enough so that you can explain it away in simple terms that then stand the best chance of being understood and ultimately acted upon.

That's it.

This is about keeping it simple, so this bit is just that.

Simple.

Sell it.

Sorry Nan.

Chapter 15 - Get The Apple Straight From The Tree

So we're nearing the end of everything I wanted to tell you and write about now and I thought this would be a good point to just throw in a couple of ideas about what I think about the future and getting fresh people interested in this game.

And I also wanted to tell you about the importance of adding social value into all this too.

Movie trivia time again first though.

The title of this chapter comes from an idea and a line in one of my all-time favourites, "The Untouchables".

COSTNER, DE NIRO, CONNERY and a young Andy GARCIA.

Brian de PALMA directs.

Script written by David MAMET.

Suits by ARMARNI.

Told you it was a favourite.

Where do you stand on Sean CONNERY being the best "Bond" by the way?

Daniel CRAIG was awesome and a local lad to where I'm from, so it's a difficult one.

DC probably tips it for me.

No naff polls on it here though.

Discuss it amongst yourselves.

Sean CONNERY does however, play a world-weary Irish beat cop in "The Untouchables". A Spanish immortal in "Highlander". A Russian submarine captain in "The Hunt For Red October" and "Indiana Jones's" Dad in the "Last Crusade".

And, all of them with a Scottish accent regardless.

So, in the legend, "Shoot From The Lip" stakes, he's well out in front.

Back to business...

So, in "The Untouchables" they are looking at ways in which they can effectively investigate and build a case against Al CAPONE.

Corruption and fear is rife, so Sean CONNERY'S character advises Elliot NESS (Kevin COSTNER) to go to the Police Academy and seek out younger officers/recruits in an effort to bring in "fresh" people.

And in doing this he tells him that,

"If you're afraid of getting a rotten apple, don't go to the barrel. Get it off the tree".

He basically has all of the good, no all the great lines in the movie, but it's this one that is relevant here.

Now, I'm not talking about this in the context of corruption obviously, but it is worth pausing and thinking on for a moment and considering if how, sometimes "experience", can have some negative effects on people.

They can pick up some bad habits and have closed minds and ideas.

The old phrase of "this is how it's always been done" springs to mind here.

There is quite a lot of this type of thinking around and some of it in the safety game too.

It is changing though and that is a good thing.

But we need to do MORE.

I really like the idea of apprenticeships.

I've done quite a bit in this area in recent times and I would definitely look to take on a proper apprentice in H&S if the right opportunity presented itself, as I think apprenticeships are a really good way for people to get into work and study at the same time. They are cost effective (always thinking salesman) and add value (one of our key phrases) for both the individual and the organisation.

There are some really good incentives out there for employers to take on apprentices and I urge you, if you're in a position to influence this, to really have a good look into it.

I've worked on some great partnership projects with clients and education providers to recruit a number of apprentices in both the construction trades and office-based roles. We carried out a decent screening and selection process and looked for people who displayed the right behaviours rather than just academic/technical ability, and I think using this process, (which, by the way I totally advocate for most appraisal/performance approaches), enabled us to pick the right people.

Their results and feedback tell us this.

Happy, motivated people, who are being mentored in both the practical ways of work, doing an actual proper job, getting paid a bit for it and also studying the theory side as well.

Now, I went to university and when I was 18 and I didn't consider any kind of apprenticeship.

Not even for a minute.

But fast forward twenty-five years (OMG) and I am really into this kind of thing and would actively encourage my own kids to consider them, if it was something that they were interested in.

And for me, what you may lose in recruiting someone with clearly less experience, you gain in a willingness to learn, develop and grow.

This investment WILL pay back, and in my opinion, many times over, against a person who perhaps is more "closed" to new ideas and taking a fresh approach.

At the time of writing this, (throughout 2021 and early 2022), I have been involved in a lot of work on social value, and in particular supporting people with employability and work experience opportunities, as well as the apprenticeship recruitment. This work has been some of the most rewarding I have ever done in my career so far.

I really, really encourage you to try and get involved with some of this if you get the chance. If you can get just one person interested and enthused, then you have made a difference and added value, so start looking at it.

I'll end this bit on that.

It made sense to me at the time to tell you about it and it is about adding value, which is, as we know by now, a key theme.

I know it's not directly safety related but it is really important and worth some thought so go and get involved where you can.

Chapter 16 - This Is The End

"This is the end my beautiful friend. The end"

"The End" by "The Doors".

Great name.

Great music.

Great look.

That song was used in the movie "Apocalypse Now" and the bit where Martin SHEEN pops his head out of the water when he's hunting down Marlon BRANDO'S character.

Crazy movie.

"The Doors" itself was a decent film too with "Iceman" in the lead role too.

I told you I'd try to pull some of these ideas together...

"Iceman".

"Talk to me Goose", remember?

Welcome to my world.

Quick last debate then about the best band(s) of the 60's.

"The Beatles" and "The Rolling Stones" are too obvious by the way, so you can't have them.

But if you think any of the below then I commend you:

"Led Zeppelin"

"Love"

"Pink Floyd" got better in the '70's.

Anyway, debate amongst yourselves. I haven't got all day.

Seriously though friends.

This is. "The End".

No big sprawling conclusions or summaries here, as that just goes against everything we've said about this whole approach and my take on it all.

You've got this far, so I think there is plenty there for you to go at and make your own minds up.

And that's all there is to it.

Keep it simple.

Keep it concise.

And keep it REAL.

Now get out there and sell it.

Shoot From The Lip.

The Safety Salesman.

Postscript

I know. I know.

That last bit was this is "The End", so what's this bit then?

Listen. Give me a break.

I've read a few real books by proper authors, and they all do this, so it must the thing to do, so we're doing it too.

Likewise, the foreword by the way.

Which, as you know, is by a real IOSH ex-President and everything, Sir James QUINN.

I can sense you're wondering how I came to bag or blag him to do it in the first place?

Well, I could tell you that there were promises of endless riches and fame beyond our wildest dreams but that would probably mean he would have to give his big medal back (which he loves), so just forget I said anything about that.

Let's just say instead that, he is top fella, who seriously, has done and continues to do, loads for this game, in a really positive and forward-looking way, especially with our veterans and someone who has inspired me on many levels.

A top-drawer bloke. End of.

The postscript thing then. I think it's meant to be a look back at the content or a review of some of the key moments or something, but I'm not going over all that again, so I'll just say this to you.

Writing this book has been a truly amazing experience for me and one I have absolutely loved doing. It's also been (if I'm really honest) some good therapy for me and I hope anyone reading it can find something useful within it.

But more so, something relatable.

If it sparks a connection, a memory, an idea or even just a laugh, then that it what I set out to do and that for me, is the job done.

And that, my friends, is the real bottom line.

Thanks for reading.

"Hasta la vista baby..."

Printed in Great Britain
by Amazon